this is
the day

sue monk kidd

THE C. R. GIBSON COMPANY
Norwalk, Connecticut 06856

Published by the C. R. Gibson Company
Norwalk, Connecticut 06856
Copyright © 1987 by Guideposts Associates
Printed in the United States of America
All rights reserved
ISBN 0-8378-1828-1

JANUARY

Behold, all things are become new.

II CORINTHIANS 5:17

 STARTING

HIGH in the mountains of North Carolina snow was falling on the roof of the little cabin. Inside, a fire burned on the grate. My husband Sandy and I were spending New Year's Eve by the warm bricks of the fireplace. Sometimes the flames leaped high with an illusive beauty, reminding me of the bright dreams for the year ahead. And then they'd turn low and brooding like sad regrets of the year past. How tenaciously our mistakes and regrets hang on...tiny stumbling blocks to the future.

Midnight drew near. "It would be nice to burn all the failures of the past year and start clean," Sandy said.

So we each got a pencil and paper and began to search within ourselves for all the unwelcome baggage we didn't want to carry into the new year. Old mistakes, bad habits, guilt feelings, burdens. My list grew long, seeming dark and heavy by the blue firelight. How, I wondered, had I managed to drag all that around for so long.

At the stroke of midnight we let our lists float down into the fire. The papers curled with brown edges, then ignited suddenly. Watching them burn, I whispered a prayer, "God, I want to start anew. Cleanse me now."

The next day, taking the shovel from the hearth, I raked the gray ashes from the fireplace and dumped them behind the cabin. Away in the clean, white morning they blew, swirling toward heaven. Gone. It was a new beginning.

Wash me and I will be whiter than snow, Lord.

 REACHING FOR TOMORROW

I ONCE spent part of a pleasant afternoon interviewing Henry Aaron, baseball's home-run king. As I climbed the steps to the stadium to keep our appointment, I paused to gaze at the bronze statue of Hank Aaron shining there in the warm Atlanta sunlight. The figure captured a dazzling moment in his career, when he slammed his record-breaking 715th home run. Standing beneath the monument, I gazed up, thinking it seemed a shame that all the cheers and exciting moments were over. Now Hank worked behind a desk for the Atlanta Braves.

I suppose history was on my mind, because the first thing I asked him was: "How do you feel when you walk past that great bronze statue of yourself every day, knowing that your playing days are behind you?"

Hank smiled across the desk. "Oh, that doesn't bother me," he replied. "I can't afford to concentrate on the past. There are new challenges and opportunities waiting every day." His words reminded me of something Paul wrote: *"...Old things are passed away; behold, all things are become new." (II Corinthians 5:17)*

Now a new year is just beginning. And it occurs to me that I have my own "bronze statues" to contend with—past victories and failures, achievements and regrets—things that need to be put behind. Each new day ahead will be filled with fresh opportunities from God.

Moving on past yesterday and reaching for tomorrow. What a wonderful way to begin this new year!

Father, help me to leave last year's guilts and glories at the door of this new year as I cross the threshold with hands outstretched to receive Your new instructions.

 # A RAINBOW MOMENT

IT was a steamy hot day down South—when the sun can burn the rubber off your sneakers. It was also the day the air conditioner quit. In 30 minutes the house was a furnace. "Come on, kids," I called. "I'll cut on the sprinkler for you."

I sat in the pathetic shade of a maple while Ann and Bob danced through the stream of water. Time oozed by like slow, hot tar. I sat there, miserable, immune to everything but the heat and what it would cost to repair the air conditioner.

Suddenly Ann squealed. "A rainbow! I made a rainbow!"

She had placed her hand over the water causing a fine spray and somehow out of the mystery of sunlight and water drops, a radiant little rainbow arched right out of her hand. My daughter stared at it, her eyes polished with wonder. And watching her childlike fascination, I wondered what had become of my own ability to turn loose of the world's seriousness for just a moment, and find pure simple delight in a tiny arc of color shining in one's hand.

I turned loose and looked around me. I noticed for the first time how the leaves and grass shimmered under a golden blanket of the sun's hot light. I reached down and felt the velvet green shape of one unique clover petal...studied the flitting ballet of a butterfly and listened to the rustling quiet that lies deep in every summer day. And as I did, something began to happen inside me, as if the child in me woke up to a world rinsed with newness. But something more. As I became aware of each creation about me, I discovered the Creator, too. Even the tiny rainbow shining in the sprinkler spelled God's name with its colors.

Awaken my childlike capacity to wonder, Lord.

FEBRUARY

*This is the day which the Lord hath
made; we will rejoice and be glad.*

PSALMS 118:24

 THE GREATEST DAY

EARLY one morning I slumped half-asleep at the breakfast table. "Another day," I muttered into my orange juice.

"Which day do you think's the greatest day of your life?" my husband asked.

"The greatest day?" I said. "Let's see, the day I was born. No, that's not it. How about the day we got married? Or the day I was baptized? Or the days the children were born?" I sank my chin into my hands. "Oh, I give up. It's too early in the morning for this."

"No, it's not," he replied. "It's perfect timing. You see, you're looking for the greatest day of your life in the wrong direction. The greatest day of your life is today."

Today? I gazed at him in surprise. And suddenly I saw that he was right. This was not just "another day." It was *the* day, the only day I had. The only day in which I could actually touch reality. A day to fill with more love than yesterday. A day to grow closer to God in. Why, it was a day bursting with marvelous possibilities.

I will always remember that particular day. For viewing it as the greatest day of my life was like putting a freshly polished pair of glasses on the face of my humdrum, nearsighted existence. That day was very special. But it was not the greatest day of life. No, today is.

Lord, help me make this day the best ever.

 RAINY DAYS

RAIN streaked the windows. It clattered on the roof like horses' hooves and surrounded the house with an impregnable gray curtain. "I hate rain," I mumbled. I'd been cooped up all day with two over-zealous children and one oversized dog. The den looked like a toy-strewn battleground and I felt like a prisoner of war.

I got on all fours and began to pick up the blocks. "I hate blocks," I said, frowning crossly. The children frowned back.

"Can we have a cookie?" asked Bob.

"Cookies make crumbs and I despise crumbs," I grumbled. They pouted at me.

"We don't have nothing to do," Bob said.

"Well, pick up your crayons!" I practically shouted.

His mouth turned down. He started to whimper. Thunder snapped overhead like a giant rubber band. The gloom inside the house deepened. I flipped on TV and heard the familiar music of "Sesame Street."

"The dog chewed up my red crayon!" Ann screamed, pointing to the carpet full of red wax.

"I hate the dog," I said.

Then suddenly, a voice on television said, "I hate puppies." I looked up to see if there was an echo in the room. But it was Oscar the Grouch, the outrageous, furry green creature who lives in a trash can, the grumbling crosspatch of Sesame Street. I watched Oscar as he went about the business of hating everything and making everybody miserable, and felt like I was looking in the mirror. I shifted my eyes to the rain-soaked window. There would always be unpleasant circumstances that I simply couldn't change. But I *could* improve the climate that surrounded them, with a few adjustments to my disposition.

I surprised the kids with a hug. "Want a cookie?" I said.

Lord, keep me from being a grouch—even on
the rainy days.

 THE GIFT

ONE summer afternoon a small barefoot girl sat on the bank of a pond with her granddaddy, fishing. He wore a straw hat. She wore a dandelion behind her ear. A wind rustled in the pines. And there was not another sound—just her granddaddy's breathing. He had left work early to bring her fishing. She knew that was not easy. For he was a busy man. He was a judge.

For just a moment the girl forgot her pole. The end splattered into the water, sending the dragonflies scurrying off their lily pad. "Whoa, fishing pole," her granddaddy said, reaching over to steady the cane pole. She giggled.

"Watch that cork," he said, his finger pointing to the water. "When our fish comes nibbling, let him have a taste, then pull."

"Yessir," she said.

Shadows crept over the water. The sun sank low. But the old man sat as still as the pines, as if time were suspended and their minutes were as countless as summer berries.

She rested her cheek against his arm. "Granddaddy, are you sure there's a fish in this pond?" she asked.

He smiled at her, his eyes sparkling behind his glasses. Evening gathered around their shoulders like an old country quilt, pulling them together.

Suddenly the cork zinged under the water with such force the girl slid down the bank. "It's a whopper!" cried her granddaddy. She dug her toes in the mud and leaned back into his arms. They pulled. Breaking through the water, erupting into the last glimmer of daylight, burst the biggest fish she had ever seen. She held up the silver fish and sucked in her breath. Her granddaddy's face beamed down at her. And neither of them spoke. They only stared at one another over the dancing fish.

The gift of that afternoon was just about the best present the child ever got. I know. For I was the little girl with the dandelion behind my ear. And the granddaddy who left work early was mine. And he taught me something priceless that day. That there are many wonderful gifts I can give those I love, but the one that lingers when all the others are gone, the one that knits the brightest threads into life, is the gift of my time—the gift of myself.

The moments I share with those I love are
the really cherished ones. Don't let me be too
busy today, Lord.

MARCH

To every thing there is a season.

ECCLESIASTES 3:1

 SPRING FEVER

TODAY I woke up with a restless feeling pulsing inside. I want to dig in the dirt and make something grow. I want to clean out my closets and paint the bedrooms and chase butterflies. I am full of stirrings and longings born sometime during the night. Every year about this time, it happens to me. Somewhere between the last breath of winter and the first green leaf, I contract "spring fever."

Suddenly I am struck by a thought. Could spring fever actually be a spiritual phenomenon? Could my hunger to grow a flower, redecorate the house and follow the flight of a newly resurrected butterfly actually be a sign of some deeper need? Could it really be a hunger for my own growth and resurrection?

I begin to hear God speaking to me, showing me how insular, barren and static my spiritual life became through the cold winter. My prayers are frozen like the January ground and my commitment seems unfocused and neglected like a cluttered closet.

So I decide. Yes…I will go and plant seeds in the earth… follow a butterfly…and clean my closets. But I will also take time to cultivate the "spring" burgeoning within my spirit. Beginning now.

Father, there is something wonderful stirring
deep within the cocoon in which I have wrapped
myself—unfurl new life in me.

PATCHWORK QUILT

MY husband's grandma had just finished sewing a rosebud pink dress. A Sunday-go-to-meeting dress, she called it. I remembered how carefully she pored over patterns while I drummed my fingers on the counter. I remembered waiting while she stroked every bolt of knit, feeling for the right cloth. Next came hours of pedaling her ancient sewing machine.

She held up the dress and smiled. "Tomorrow I'll wear it to church," she announced, draping the dress over the ironing board. The iron was old and overheated. In seconds a large brown scorch seared onto the soft rosebud pink.

Looking it over, Grandma pulled out her scissors and cut the dress into small squares. She tucked the little pile of squares into her sewing basket. I knew she meant them for a quilt.

On cold wind-whistling nights, whenever I draw up the quilt of rosebud pink squares that warms my bed, I ask God if there is a little pile of disappointments and sorrows in my life that I can patch into something good.

Father, when I stand in the middle of shredded plans and dreams, teach me how to take these remnants and use them for something good.

CHANGING

ONCE I felt especially frustrated by my inability to stamp out a particular little habit in my life. I had tried countless times to break it, without success. *What's the use? I can't change,* I thought. *It's simply the way I am.*

Later that day I took a walk and found myself beside a beautiful old church. As I looked up, filled with admiration for the graceful brick tower, my eyes fell on a tree growing just inside the church yard. It was a striking tree, half autumn red, half summer green. I had caught it in perfect transition. Reaching up, I plucked a leaf and studied it, fascinated by the process that was gradually transforming its colors. Patiently, quietly, the leaf had yielded itself to the mysterious work of God's design.

As I stood there musing, I began to gather hope. If God designed such a miraculous capacity for change into the leaf, surely He did so for me too. I also could be transformed! But first, like the leaf, I must yield myself to God—with complete trust and patience—and offer no resistance to His work within me.

There beneath the cool shadows of the autumn tree, I tucked the near-crimson leaf into my pocket, a reminder that no one should ever give up on himself. With God's plan at work in our lives, we can all be changed—just as surely as the changing of the seasons!

Help me to see Your design for my life, Father,
and then follow it.

APRIL

Make a joyful noise unto God.

PSALMS 66:1

 **HELLO JESUS**

THE congregation was gathered in the small church for worship. While waiting for the service to begin, I let my thoughts roam. In front of me a little girl, maybe three years old, hummed a Sunday-school tune to herself...Carol, a dear friend of mine, was wearing a pretty new dress...Helen's deep suntan really became her...I noticed two light bulbs out in the big chandelier up toward the balcony....

Looking at my watch, I shifted in my seat and then let my mind drift again...until the child in front of me, no longer humming, suddenly shouted out in excitement, her shrill little voice striking like a clap of thunder in the quiet church: "Look, Mama!" She pointed to the Good Shepherd stained-glass window above the altar. "There's Jesus. Hello, Jesus! Jesus, hello!"

For me it was a moment of pure illumination. Here was the smallest one in our midst teaching us that waiting-time in church is precious time...not a time to fritter away our thoughts on idle trivia. The tot's attention had been focused on thoughts of Him...she had been *expecting* to meet Him...and, in her own way, she did!

We, too, while we wait in church, should be turning our thoughts toward meeting our Lord...preparing our reception—readying ourselves to say simply, "Hello, Father. Here I am." And then we too will meet our Master.

Dear Father, I am ready. My heart awaits You.

 JOY

ONE day my small daughter painted her very own "stained-glass" picture—a plastic sign that spelled the word "joy." She filled in the panes with translucent purples, blues and reds. I propped it in the kitchen window, where it caught the sun's rays and reflected a rainbow of light into the room. It was almost like looking at joy itself. Every morning when I arrived in the kitchen, there it was—joy streaming in through the window.

But one morning I walked into the kitchen in a dark mood. The joy sign made such a contrast to my feelings that impulsively I reached up and pulled the curtain across it. *Like snuffing out a candle*, I thought. All the colorful brightness it had smiled into the room disappeared.

Later as I crossed the back yard to empty the trash, I glanced up at the window, expecting to see the sign shining as gaily as it had from the other side. But a curious thing had happened. The word "joy," usually so brilliant, leaned against the sill dark and dull. The sun was still beaming down into the little piece…but why were the once-vibrant colors so downcast? Then I saw it. The curtain I had drawn now served as a backdrop that prevented the light from filtering through. Shining *in* was not enough to light it; the sun had to shine *through*.

People are like stained glass, I thought. *We're not meant to let God's light simply shine in on us—we must let it shine through us. Otherwise joy will darken and fade away.* As I returned inside, the kitchen curtain was not the only thing I had resolved to open wide. It occurred to me that there were a few curtains of my own, drawn between myself and others, that needed opening as well.

Dear Lord, please let Your light shine through me…and onto others.

 LABELS

ONE morning my friend stopped at an intersection behind a bright blue car. It was one of those mornings when the dogwood was bursting open everywhere and the air was heavy with gardenia and God was in His heaven. As Joel sat there, he noticed the car in front had a bumper sticker plastered across the back window. It said, "Honk if you love Jesus." Now Joel is not given to that sort of thing. But he felt so gloriously wonderful from the beauty of the day, and the idea of loving Jesus gave him such a lift, that he looked at that bumper sticker and said, "Oh, why not?"

He tapped his horn and smiled through the windshield. He expected a happy honk back. Instead a man with a dark scowl jerked his head out the window and yelled, "Hey Mac, hold your horses!" Suddenly the day turned sour. Joel's comment was, "If he's going to wear the label, he ought to live up to it."

We all have our labels, like invisible bumper stickers plastered across our lives. Christian—I've stamped that one on my life. Today someone is bound to pull up behind me and notice. He might even reach out to me because of it. I must try not to disappoint him. I'll give him a happy honk back.

Help me to live my label, as well as wear it, Lord.

THE WALK

OUR eight-year-old spaniel, Captain Marvel, was over-weight and in need of exercise. My nine-year-old daughter Ann dug out the dog leash. "Mama, let's take Captain for a walk," she said.

I didn't usually take walks, but at her urging I agreed.

The three of us struck out along our little neighborhood street. "Look, a squirrel!" squealed Ann. "Oh, Mama, see how yellow those flowers are!"... "Why is there moss on trees?"... "That cloud looks like a rhinoceros." She constantly drew my attention to the things around us. Things I knew were there, but never looked at.

Cloud, sun, tree bark, grasshoppers, the smell of jonquils, the green in the grass. Something began to well up in me—a sense of Presence of the One who had made all this. The line of an old hymn flickered through my head. "In the rustling grass, I hear Him pass."

We walked on. I began trying to discover God through the ordinary things along the path, for I was finding that the sights and sounds in God's creation could be signposts pointing to Him, like voices speaking of His mystery and beauty. And it was not like trudging through a familiar old neighborhood at all. It was like strolling into a brand new awareness of God.

Try taking a "daily walk with God" in which you take time to practice His Presence by seeing Him in the small and splendid things around you. Why, it could even spill over into your walk through the rest of the year!

Dear God, let me walk with You and seek You
in both the ordinary and extraordinary that
dot my path.

MAY

Draw nigh to God.

JAMES 4:8

LISTENING

ONE Sunday evening before the church service began, I made my way up three flights of stairs to a little prayer room. It sat like a crow's nest atop the church, a quiet alcove next to the balcony. When I entered, I found the little room caught in that brief, peculiar time just before the sun disappears, when the air is thick and warm and golden. The stained-glass window was at its luminous best. And not a sound floated up to mar the deep peace of the little alcove.

I sat down on the front bench. A gold cross gleamed brightly on the altar before me. I bowed my head, remembering the haunting words that had prompted me to climb the stairs for a few stolen moments alone with God. Words I had read the day before: *"God speaks to us every day, but we do not listen."* Did He? I wondered if even now God was speaking to me. Had I missed the sound of His coming into my life? I waited, my head bowed, listening to the empty, silent space.

The minutes swept by and the shadows became long and soft-hued. I looked up finally and was startled by what I saw. Directly before me shone the altar cross, and my own image was reflecting from its surface. My eyes stared back at me from the lateral crosspiece. I was captured in the cross with a strangely balanced precision, the reflection as clear and sharp as though in a mirror.

"Are you speaking to me, God?" I whispered into the glowing silence. The last bit of light filtering from the window caused my image on the cross to gleam even more brightly for an instant. Then the air was filled with the unspoken message of redemption—Jesus died for me. For ME. I belonged on the cross, not Him. And yet He took my place.

I climbed down from the prayer loft, believing. Yes, God speaks. For He came to me through my own face shining in the center of a cross.

Jesus, today let me be worthy of Your sacrifice.

I WANT TO BE WITH YOU

ONE evening I drew up the rocking chair and turned on the lamp. Soon I was rocking and humming over a piece of needlepoint. Suddenly I got one of those feelings of being watched. Looking up, I saw my five-year-old son staring at me from the doorway. He sauntered over and crawled into my lap.

"What do you want?" I asked.

"Nothing," he said. "I just want to be with you."

He laid his head on my arm, content just to be near me, to curl up in my circle of lamplight and delight in my presence. What joy for me!

There are times when I feel that way about God. I slip into His presence, not because I want something, not because I'm in trouble again. But because I simply want to be with Him. I want to climb into the warm pool of light around Him and revel in all that He is.

Do you need a tender moment in God's lap today?

Lord, I come into Your presence, not with a want list, but yearning only to be near You.

THE COUNSELOR

WHEN we were eleven years old, my friend Connie and I went to a very "outback" Girl Scout camp. Upon arriving we found that we had been assigned to a wonderful counselor named Robbie. But we soon discovered that we'd been assigned chores too—peeling potatoes, scrubbing cabin floors, and cleaning latrines. Even on our pleasure hikes we were constantly enlisted to gather firewood, clear away rocks, or carry equipment.

We noticed that the girls closest to Robbie always had the greatest number of chores to do. It seemed that whoever was handiest was volunteered. Therefore, on future hikes we developed the artful strategy of walking at a safe distance. We didn't fall so far back that we might become lost, but neither did we stay so close that we might become involved in any hard work. Staying at a safe distance took a lot of finesse, but we pulled it off for about a week, escaping all sorts of tasks.

Then one sunny afternoon we saw the other girls sitting in a circle under the boughs of a big, spreading tree—laughing and sharing delicious secrets with Robbie, who sat in their midst. We stood to one side by ourselves and watched. We felt apart, excluded, *alone*. That's when it dawned on us that we had also escaped the joy of forming a close and happy friendship with our counselor. So we moved nearer to the circle, and soon we were once again hauling firewood. But closing ranks with our counselor, we made our last week at camp a truly rewarding experience.

I think that the closer we stay to Christ, the deeper is our awareness of the Gospels' true demands. But only when we stand back, we find that we are alone, out of His circle. It's His friendship that makes life abundant and enriching.

We have only to stay close.

Keep me close, Lord, to the fire of Your love.

 DRY CUP DAYS

I WAS a wreck! My son had driven a grocery cart through the cake mix display at the supermarket, my daughter had bathed eight stuffed animals in a tub of water, and the dog had turned over three newly-potted geraniums on the rug. I could go on, but I won't depress you. I was having one of my dry cup days.

I get them. Maybe you do, too. They are the days that leave me empty as a dry cup. You know the ones—ringing phones, children's quarrels, spilled grape juice, overdue library books and a frantic tangle of errands and demands. All together these little frustrations can wear a hole in my day through which peace and perspective drain away.

You know what I did? I dropped everything and carried my dry cup to an armchair in the bedroom. Hidden away from the distractions, I closed my eyes and held up my cup to God for a refill. I didn't think of the 40 boxes of cake mix crashing down, or the water-logged animals, or the carpet full of potting soil. I thought about God. I imagined Him pouring His love and peace and strength down upon me. There, in those few silent moments, He filled my cup. Filled it up. And I returned to the little human things of my life, my cup brimming with peace.

On the dry cup days, Lord, help me to seek
a quiet corner for a refill.

 THE CONCH

I CUPPED the small conch shell to my ear. Sitting very still, I listened for the sound within its labyrinths. Then I heard it—the faint and haunting echo buried deep inside, the whispering voice of the ocean.

And sitting there with my back to the world's clamor, I realized that I was hearing one of the sounds hidden deep within our universe.

Are these tiny, secret sounds like little messages? I wondered later.

Like the *"still, small voice"* of God? How often God's voice is like the sound buried deep inside the conch shell. Only when I turn aside and become still, cupping my ear to the ground of God's being, can I hope to hear His gentle whisper.

Today might be a good day to try...

Teach me to spend time alone with
You, Lord...listening.

JUNE

O Lord, how manifold are thy works!…things…both small and great.

PSALMS 104: 24, 25

 LIGHTNING BUGS

MY mother and I sat on the front porch of our house in Georgia, watching the darkness creep in. Out of nowhere a mysterious yellow twinkling appeared in the night, tiny flashes of incandescence dipping beneath the pines.

"Want to catch some lightning bugs?" Mama asked.

Capture that magic? Could it be done? Mother looked at me, bounced off the steps, and fetched a mason jar, its lid pierced with holes. We walked barefoot into the darkness, following the flickering pathways of light. Mama cupped her hands and lunged. "Look," she said, making a peep hole into her hand. With my face pressed against her thumbs, I caught my first close-up glimpse of a lightning bug.

The jar soon filled with lights. And when Mama tucked me in that night, she placed it beside my bed. Long after everyone else was asleep, I was still awake watching the golden lights flare in the darkness.

Now, so many years later, I have forgotten most of the toys that filled my room. But the night Mama and I caught lightning bugs and made them into a night light is imprinted on my mind.

Mama with her mason jar taught me that God filled the

world with small wonders. There is so much ordinary magic dancing around your back yard waiting to be shared with someone.

Lord, today help me to take time for a small wonder.

 DAWN

DARKNESS draped the shadow of the mountain across the valley. Barely visible were jagged tree-lined peaks rising high into the night. I had ventured out of our little rented cabin to catch the dawn. (I cannot resist seeing the sun rise over the mountains, so at least once during every mountain vacation I drag myself out of bed and sit beneath the fading stars and wait.)

I sat on a bundle of pine straw and watched a pink light climbing up the back side of the mountain growing brighter and brighter.

Then before my eyes the fiery rim of the sun crested the cliffs. It shattered the last traces of night like a mirror, sending shards of brilliance into the valley. I rose to my feet wanting to shout—*Look...oh, look! Here is the glory of God!*

I don't know about you, but moments like these are far too rare in my life. In them we begin to "live" the last line of the Lord's Prayer—*For thine is the kingdom and the power and the glory, forever!* In making it part of our lives, we must take some time to celebrate God's majesty and goodness around us. Then we will pause and recognize His Godhood in all things and rejoice in His kingdom.

Today, let us lift up our hearts in praise. For what can be more thrilling, more wondrous than being alive in a world spilling over with God's power and glory?

Father, You have taught us how to pray—and live.
And we praise Your name, and Your kingdom, and
Your power, and Your glory. Amen.

# IN HIS IMAGE

I WAS leafing through one of several books about the sea that I had brought along for my children to read at the beach.

There are 85,000 varieties of sea animals! the little book said. Creatures with ten legs. A scallop with two rows of blue eyes. A whale as long as a boxcar. A grasshopper fish that jumps along the ocean floor.

The ocean—the great brewing pot for God's imagination.

"What are you reading?" my son asked.

"*Your* book," I replied, holding up a page that showed a little boy on the beach surrounded by all sorts of marine life—anemones, sea turtles, an electric eel. "Just look at these creatures God made!" I said. "Which one do you like best?"

He studied the picture, his face breaking into an impish little grin. "The boy!" he answered.

I was surprised. *Of course, of course,* I thought. Of all the creatures God made, His imagination reached a height when He made man. I lowered the book and studied the people on the beach. Perhaps I needed to look at the human family with new eyes, to see each person as the marvelous creature he is...and most of all, as a tiny portrait of God's own image.

Lord, help me to appreciate anew Your world of wonders—and especially Your human creation.

 # VIEW FROM ABOVE

I WAS 20,000 feet in the air, my face pressed against the oval window of an airplane. Beyond, an infinite blueness blanketed the world with lonely space. My four-year-old son sat in my lap, his shaggy brown hair nestled against my shoulder.

The nose of the plane dipped. We began our descent. "In a moment we'll see a big city from the plane," I said.

We squeezed our faces into the little window and suddenly there it was, far, far below, gleaming in the sun like a child's miniature blocks. "Do you see the tiny people way down on the ground?" I asked. Bob nodded.

As he watched the ant-sized people, he asked, "Mama, is that what God sees when He looks down from heaven?"

A God's-eye view of the world? I thought of all the vastness God could see. A planet with four billion people, spinning in a universe with a hundred million galaxies. Suddenly, I felt small and insignificant…an ant-sized speck at the end of God's vision.

Bob tucked his head beneath my chin. His hair tickled my neck and some words of Jesus drifted to mind. *"The very hairs of your head are all numbered."* *(Matthew 10:30)* How could I forget? God deals up close and personally with every person. I turned to my son. "When God looks down on the world, He sees us so closely, He can count every hair on our heads. That's how special and near we are to Him."

"Wow!" Bob whispered, wide-eyed with wonder.

I smiled. That was my feeling, exactly.

When I feel tiny and insignificant, lost in
the vastness of everything, remind me that in
Your eyes, I am special.

JULY

By His light I walked through darkness.

JOB 29:3

 THE DOOR OF HOPE

IT'S a dark, gloomy Saturday, perhaps like that Saturday long ago when the crucified Jesus lay in a tomb.

I pause just outside the chapel, listening to the deep, hollow silence ringing through the dim church, and I am reminded of how silent and dark and still it was within His Saturday tomb. Low, rumbling thunder threatens the sky outside. Then I notice a passage near the stairs to the balcony. Seeking a place in which to meditate, I go through and into a small, beautifully furnished parlor. On one wall there is a splendid stained-glass window. Jesus stands there before a door, a shining lantern in His hand. Beneath is the inscription: *"I am the light of the world."*

Settling on a sofa behind the window, I place myself inside the scene, standing in the shadows to one side. The lantern in His hand swings to and fro gently, spreading long fingers of light into the distance. A small opening cut high in the door behind Him reveals nothing but darkness on the other side. I'm perplexed. What lies beyond this dark door? And now—but wait. Where is He going? Christ is pulling open the big gloomy door and stepping through, where He is engulfed in the darkness beyond. "Come back, my Lord!" I cry out, forgetting myself for the moment.

And then I wait, watching the door with a terrible sense of sadness. But look! Something unexpected is happening. A faint light begins to flicker from the other side. It grows in intensity until at last a brilliant radiance pours forth from that opening high in the door.

As I sit here gazing into the flood of light, my meditation gradually comes to a close. I know that this window, hidden away here in the little parlor, is a symbolic picture of that Saturday of long ago...for then too it seemed that Christ had been swallowed up in the darkness of the "other side." And what had resembled a dark and forbidding door is actually the door of hope, from which His light shines forth, just as it did from behind the stone that sealed His tomb in the garden outside Jerusalem.

I let these thoughts sift and settle in my mind as I depart into the misting rain outside. What message has this window given me? Something about hoping when there is no reason to hope? Something about trusting in the light of God that comes to us when things seem bleakest? Something about clinging to the promise of victory springing out of defeat?

Yes, all of that. And more.

Lord Jesus, I stand here before Your door of hope.
May I enter?

 LETTING GO

I HAD found little relief from the burden I was carrying around. Someone I loved was very ill and I could actually feel a heaviness within myself from the weight of it. I had prayed and prayed—but without very much peace.

Late one night, unable to sleep, I slipped into my little girl's room to make sure that she was covered. The night light glowed through the organdy ruffle of her canopied bed, where she lay fast asleep. And just as I suspected, her blanket had been kicked to the foot of the bed. As I drew the cover over her, I noticed that she clutched a half-eaten grape lollipop in her hand. A birthday present from her grandmother that she had carried around all day. Now the candy made a sticky purple splotch on the pillowcase, and a few strands of my daughter's hair were stuck to it.

Why didn't she get rid of this before going to bed? I thought. Of course I knew why. She was reluctant to trust anything so precious out of her sight. Her little fingers were still wound tightly around the stick, and I had to pry them away one by one. And as I freed them, I began to see a small lesson in all of this. A fragile lesson that tugged at me. A lesson in learning how to let go.

No wonder I had found so little peace in my concern over my burden. I had been praying with my fingers wrapped tightly around it, afraid to trust anything so precious to anyone else. So there by the bed I bowed my head and, uncurling my fingers one by one, I let go of my burden, transferring it from my hands to God's.

Still holding the big purple lollipop, I bent down and kissed my daughter's face. Her gift…my burden…they were in good hands.

Lord, help me leave my burdens with You when I pray. For there is no better place for them.

 A CARING FATHER

AS night settled silently upon the sprawling hospital, I prepared to make nursing rounds on the ninth floor pediatric wing. Tiptoeing into a darkened ward, I beamed my flashlight on the sleeping children. A tiny kitten-like whimper drifted from the corner bed. I turned my pool of light on Amy. Her pink daisied nightgown quivered under the sheets. Her brown eyes spilled over with tears. Tomorrow Amy would lose her tonsils.

"What's the matter?" I asked, wrapping my arm around her.

"It's dark and I am all by myself," she said.

"Then why don't I stay with you?" I said.

Though she tried very hard to be brave, my presence could not stop her tears. Finally, fearing she would get no rest, I gave her a sedative. But even the medicine was useless. Her tears grew into sobs.

In desperation I phoned her father at home. Soon he stood by Amy's bed. She slipped her small hand into her father's. With her hand anchored in his, she closed her eyes and slept.

When you stumble into the dark places of life, all by yourself, there is a caring Father beside you. His hand reaches down, outstretched and strong. Reach up. Clasp hold your hand in His...There is the only peace!

Father, I slip my hand into Yours and
rest securely.

 # GOD'S CHURCH

SEVERAL years ago devastating tornadoes lashed through South Carolina, creating unbelievable destruction. Little towns and communities around us appeared to have been bombed.

About 5:17 P.M. the monstrous black funnel hit St. Luke's Episcopal Church in Newberry, our neighbor to the east. The roof was peeled off like a piece of paper and blown away. Most of the church was wrecked—walls, pews, windows.

I followed the news about the little one-room church in the newspaper and on television. Like everything else about the tornado's havoc, this struck me as a terrible tragedy. The loss of an entire church.

On Sunday after the tornado came, the parishioners gathered in the shell. I watched on television and saw them all standing together, singing. The priest lifted the communion bread and wine. It was then I saw it—the people had not lost a church, only a building. The church was the body of Christ. It was those believers gathered together, sharing bread and wine.

I learned a lesson that fills my heart with hope. No matter what storms come, no matter how black the sky turns, the church of Christ will not be destroyed.

Your church lives in us, Lord. Thank You!

# AUGUST

*For, behold, the kingdom of God is
within you.*

LUKE 17:21

YOU CAN DO IT

MY father always believed in me more than I believed in myself. When I was growing up, I would ask his advice on matters that seemed beyond me. "Daddy, do you think I can climb that tree?" I asked when I was small, pointing to an enormous oak.

He nodded right away. "Sure you can," he said.

When I was fourteen, I asked, "Daddy, do you believe I could make the basketball team?"

He thought it over for a moment. And then he said, "You can do it."

But I particularly remember a day when I was seventeen. I let him read my English theme and then, trying to sound nonchalant, I said, "Daddy, do you suppose...maybe one day I could be a writer?" I waited, swallowing hard.

He smiled at me. "You can do it," he said. "You can."

Maybe we all need somebody like my father. Someone to affirm our capacities. Someone to help us reach just a little higher than we might ordinarily reach. For God has given us far more potential than most of us ever dare to use. And the key of affirmation often helps to unlock it. My father knew that. And today—with my own children now, and with my family and friends—I want to use that key, too.

Help me always to draw out the very best
in others.

 RIPPLES

THOMAS à KEMPIS spent his life remote in a monastery in the Netherlands. There he wrote a collection of meditations called the *Imitation of Christ*, which he probably thought would never go beyond the monastery walls. Yet three hundred years later the captain of a slave ship found a copy of this little monk's work aboard his vessel.

During a long voyage, Captain John Newton read the small volume. It had a profound effect upon his life and eventually Newton gave his life to Christ and became a minister. He won many men to Christ. One of them, a member of the British parliament, after his conversion put forth a bill outlawing slave traffic in the British Empire.

The *Imitation of Christ* has changed the entire world. And somewhere behind it all there was only a humble monk quietly writing down his thoughts, never dreaming that they might someday circle the earth.

Now I believe that everything we say and do matters. Nothing we give is too small for God to use—a boy's lunch of loaves and fish, a monk's little volume of words, or simply someone's tiny deed of kindness. The next time you are tempted to think that your small deed is of little consequence, remember: In God's hands it is like the proverbial pebble tossed into the pond. Its ripple may travel much farther than you might ever expect.

May I never become discouraged over doing little
things for Your glory, God.

A TREASURE HUNT

"WANT to go on a treasure hunt?" I asked my children one lazy autumn afternoon. Earlier I had buried a treasure in the back yard beside a rosebush. It was nothing more than a cigar box containing a couple of improvised certificates redeemable at the ice-cream store. The children jumped up with excitement and dashed off to the back yard.

"Am I getting hot or cold?" Bob called as he climbed up the maple tree.

"Cold—freezing cold," I told him.

"What about me? Am I getting close?" Ann asked, following some clues leading toward the rosebushes.

I smiled. "You're getting warm."

Soon the dirt was flying out of the rose garden as they tunneled into the earth with their sandbox shovels. With more glee than I had envisioned, they discovered their buried treasure.

It occurs to me that perhaps God, with His infinite concern for our welfare, has also buried a treasure—inside each and every person. A gift—a talent—a special ability. And all of life just might be a treasure hunt.

One day when my children are older, I shall remind them of the autumn day when they searched for a treasure buried by the rosebush. And I shall remind them too of the treasures buried within themselves. Treasures placed there by God.

Indeed, we each have a quest.

Father, help me to discover my gifts from You,
for You.

 ## ACTS OF LOVE

WHENEVER I face a particularly difficult or unpleasant task and my motivation level is hovering near empty, I try to remind myself of a little story that I heard years ago.

An American tourist was walking down a street in India when she came upon a young missionary nurse who was washing the legs and feet of an old man who had leprosy. The tourist was repelled by the sight.

"I wouldn't do that for a million dollars!" she exclaimed.

The young nurse looked up at her and smiled. "Neither would I," she said. "But I *would* do it for Christ."

For Christ. That is the only motivation for any task we ever face. Somehow, when we perform our earthly chores in His name, they are not chores but acts of love. If you face an especially hard or unpleasant job today, why not try to do it for Christ?

Help me to become a servant just for You, Jesus.

 THE QUESTION

RECENTLY I read a story attributed to Rabbi Joseph Liebermann. In the tale, the rabbi falls asleep one night and has a dream. In the dream he dies and goes to stand before the Judgment Seat of God. As he waits for God to speak, he fears that the Lord will ask him, "Why weren't you a Moses...or a David...or a Solomon?" But God surprises him. He simply asks, "Why weren't you Rabbi Liebermann?"

Now I've read a lot about Mother Teresa and her selfless work in India; I've noted the lives of dedicated Christians throughout the world; and I've observed those around me who seem to accomplish so much for God. And next to all these I've felt myself ordinary and inadequate.

Sometimes I've even longed to do as they have done.

But the rabbi's story has set me straight. When my life is over, perhaps God will ask me why I wasn't Mother Teresa. But he might ask, "Why weren't you Sue Kidd? Why didn't you offer the world that special gift I gave only to *you*—the gift of yourself?"

I don't think I'm going to wait for Him to ask the question. Instead, I'm asking it of myself today.

Each of us has his own unique song to sing, his own particular gift to bring to the world. Even me! Even you!

Yes, Father, You can count on me.

SEPTEMBER

*It is more blessed to give than
to receive.*

ACTS 20:35

 ## THE GOOD-DEED COIN

THE bell rang. Children streamed from the school and out into the falling rain. I sat in my car out front waiting to pick up my son.

A little girl hurried by, with a large stack of books and a lunch box. Suddenly her books toppled to the ground. Then almost as quickly a boy stopped, bent down and picked them up.

I was surprised. Seldom had I seen such chivalry in my school days. The girl smiled at him and rushed on. Then something peculiar happened. The boy reached in his left pocket and pulled out something gold and shiny. Like a large coin. He held it up a second, then quickly dropped it into his right pocket.

A few weeks later on Christmas morning, my son opened a small gift from a friend. Inside was the same kind of shiny gold coin I'd seen in the boy's hand. On it were engraved these words: "Secretly transfer me to your right pocket each day after your good turn has been done." On the opposite side was the Boy Scout insignia. All at once I understood. It was a good-deed coin.

A few days later I went out and bought a Boy Scout coin for myself. For surely the spirit of the good-deed coin should be in every pocket.

*Oh, Lord, keep me busy with the currency
of kindness.*

 # A HANDFUL OF GIVING

IT was one of those gentle Georgia days on Granddaddy's farm, when the sun played behind the clouds, casting hazy orange shadows across the fields. I was picking cotton. I was only seven and the burlap sack I pulled was lots bigger than I was. But I'd begged Granddaddy for the chance to pick and he'd given in.

The cotton field stretched out ahead of me shiny and green and freckled with white. There were lots of pickers in the field. They were paid by the pound, so their hands moved fast. They could skin a bush of its fluffy white balls before I could scratch my nose. Their sacks were growing fat. Mine was unmistakably thin. I wanted to quit. That's when an old black woman idled up beside me, her hair tied in a faded red bandana. "Mind if I pick with you?" she asked.

"No, ma'am," I said. "I don't guess so."

Her fingers worked like music down the row. But she did a curious thing. Every time she dropped a handful of cotton in her sack, she dropped one in mine as well. "One for you and one for me," she said.

My bag grew plump. I began to smile. But I was puzzled. So when we got to the plum tree shade at the fence, I said, "Why are you putting a handful in my sack each time you put one in yours?"

Her crinkled face smoothed out into a wide smile. "Child, don't you know your Bible? Don't you know the place where it says, *'Freely ye have received, freely give'*? *(Matthew 10:8)* Remember this and don't forget—for every handful you take in life, that means you've got one to give."

And the child didn't forget. For sometimes when the taking in my life outweighs the giving, I remember, and I try to balance it up...a handful of giving for every handful of taking.

> *Lord, as I pull my little sack of need through this day, let me remember: One for You and one for me.*

THE IMPULSIVE KINDNESS

"IF you could have been any person in the Bible, who would you choose?" I asked the woman in the crimson sweater. It was a little game we played to pass time on the tour bus. "Hmmm," she said, gazing past the window. Flat-roofed houses came into view. We were coming to Bethany—the little hideaway where Jesus spent His last nights. "I'd like to have been the woman in Bethany who did the impulsive kindness for Jesus," she said. "The one who poured the precious perfume on His head."

I smiled. Such an extravagant act of love that was. It had happened on Tuesday, an exhausting day for Jesus. He had faced long, grueling attempts by the Jewish leaders to ensnare Him. Finally, as the hills turned purple with dusk, He had trudged wearily up the Mount of Olives to Bethany, to the home of Simon the leper for a quiet dinner. And suddenly, out of nowhere…a woman and her perfume. She anointed Jesus with tenderness, acting on the impulse of love…without counting the cost.

The bus jarred to a stop. We filed into the narrow streets of Bethany. The souvenir salesmen pressed around us, along with a few ragged children. I shooed them away. From the corner of my eye I saw the woman in the crimson sweater beside a shivering little girl. Suddenly—I could hardly believe it—the woman whisked off her lovely sweater and placed it tenderly around the girl's shoulders. Then I remembered her wish—"I'd like to have been the woman in Bethany who did the impulsive kindness for Jesus." And there in Bethany, whether she knew it or not…she had her wish.

This is a day for extravagant love. Help me to
share a bit without counting the cost.

# GIVING TO OTHERS

NOT long ago I came across a little story written by Theodor Reik, the well-known psychologist. It was the true story of the courtship of Moses Mendelssohn, grandfather of the famous German composer.

Moses Mendelssohn, it seems, was a small and misshapen hunchback. One day he traveled to Hamburg and visited with a merchant who had a beautiful daughter named Frumtje. Moses fell deeply in love with Frumtje. But she avoided him and even seemed frightened by his grotesque hump.

On the last day of his visit he climbed the stairs to her room to say good-bye. She sat, busy with her needlework, her face glowing with an almost celestial beauty. At his appearance Frumtje looked down at the floor. Mendelssohn's heart ached. He tried to draw her into conversation and slowly led around to the subject that filled his mind. "Do you believe marriages are made in heaven?" he asked timidly.

"Yes," she replied. "And do you?"

"Yes, of course," he said. "You see, in heaven at the birth of each boy, the Lord calls out, 'This boy should get this girl for a wife, and that boy should marry that girl.' And when I was born, my future wife was thus announced. But in my case, the Lord also added, 'But alas, his wife will have a terrible hump.'

"At that moment I called, 'Oh Lord, a girl who is humpbacked would be a tragedy. Please, Lord, give the hump to me and let her be beautiful.'"

And the girl, deeply moved, stretched out her hand for Mendelssohn's and later became his faithful and loving wife.

When I read that story I began to think of my own relationships. How long had it been since I'd done some unselfish act—some loving, sacrificial act that seemed to whisper, "Give the hump to me and let her be beautiful." *Far too long*, I thought.

Oh Lord, help me to reach for the heights of unselfishness in my relationships.

# OCTOBER

Love one another, as I have loved you.

JOHN 15:12

 REACHING OUT

WHILE clipping the long tassels of English ivy around our house with electric clippers, I accidentally caught two of my fingers in the blades. My husband whisked me to the emergency room where a kind nurse took my blood pressure and a sympathetic secretary asked me about insurance. But mostly I sat there alone holding my wound, biting my lip hoping to ease the pain. No matter how many people around me were active in concerned ways, it seemed no one really understood how alone and hurt I was feeling.

Across the room, an elderly woman appeared with a large bandage around her hand. She spotted me and came over. "Cut yourself?" she asked.

I nodded. "With hedge clippers."

Then she looked at me with a compassionate spirit that seemed to see deep inside me. "Bless your heart, you're hurting badly," she said. She leaned over and patted my knee and then left. Somehow after that, the waiting and hurting seemed easier.

Later a nurse said of the woman, "She cut her hand and had to have stitches. Kinda like you." That explained a lot. She, more than anyone, understood how I really felt.

Sometimes the most we can do for someone who's hurting is

to give them the gift of understanding that comes from the deep place where we might once have been, and with compassion acknowledge their pain, "You're hurting badly, aren't you?"

Lord, there is always someone who is going through what I have suffered. Help me to reach out to him.

 ## BEING NEEDED

MY friend had a pile of freshly-mended clothes on the front seat of her car. I noticed that a few buttons had been sewed back on with mismatched threads and the hems repaired with uneven stitches. "Who on earth did the repair work on these clothes?" I asked.

My friend smiled. "My neighbor," she answered. "She's eighty years old and lives alone."

"But you're a fantastic seamstress. You could do a much better job than this," I said.

"Oh, probably so. But my neighbor needs to be needed far more than these clothes need to be perfect."

Lord, remind me today to give someone the treasure of being needed.

 ## THE TOUCH

I CLINKED my medicine tray down beside Mr. Kelsy's hospital bed. I liked to pause in his room for a patch of conversation in the course of my busy nurse's shift. I was leaning on his bed, listening to his lively plans for retirement, when the bad news came. Within a few seconds Mr. Kelsy's future seemed shaky at best. The doctor's face hinted that the news was grim the moment he walked in. "You need immediate surgery," he said. "I'm sorry, but we really should operate right away."

When the doctor left, Mr. Kelsy stared at the bed in

stunned silence. Something painful hung in the air and Mr. Kelsy was trembling. I wanted to comfort him but there were no words. Nothing but silence. Absently I placed my hand on his shoulder, while rummaging my mind for the right words. I was at a loss. Was there nothing I could do to soothe his fears?

Imperceptibly, the shoulder beneath my hand had stopped trembling. Mr. Kelsy smiled up at me. "Thank you," he said.

Thank you? For what? I stared at my hand on his shoulder. Could one little touch communicate so much? Only a touch?

I have since learned never to underestimate the remarkable power of touch. It can speak eloquent words of love. It can say, "I'm sorry," "I care," "I understand," or simply, "I'm here." Sometimes a touch communicates in a way more vibrant and poetic than a string of polished syllables.

Once Jesus stretched out His hand and touched an untouchable leper. Only a touch. But such love.

Lord, help me to love someone today with a touch.

 THE BOUQUET

THE girls marched into the nursing home loaded down with homemade paper flowers. "Smile and tell the patients you're from the church," I instructed. They scattered into the rooms, handing out red-and-yellow bouquets of cheer.

As the girls gathered back in the hall, I noticed a wheelchair parked in the corner. Huddled in it was a woman with crooked fingers and twisted feet. How eagerly she watched the girls! I gave her a look that said, sorry, the flowers are gone, and we hurried back to the church.

Leaving the church for home, my eyes fell upon a clump of red and yellow near the door. One last bouquet, dropped behind. *Oh, no, Lord! Don't ask me to go back to deliver that,* I thought.

But I was in charge and I knew I had to. I remembered the eager face of the woman in the wheelchair. Reluctantly I scooped up the bouquet and returned to the nursing home. Still feeling some annoyance, I placed the flowers in her lap. Her eyes turned misty. "Bless you," she said, "oh, bless you."

As I watched her try to tighten her fingers about the stems, quite unexpectedly, my heart, too, was filled with joy...to the very brim.

Thank You, Father, for the rewards that kindness always brings.

 ## SUNSHINE LADY

NO one knew exactly who she was. She always came in quietly, unexpectedly, always to the same small corner of need—the hospital's pediatric wing. Invariably when she left, there was an anonymous path of sunshine wherever she had walked. I suppose that's why we nurses called her "sunshine lady."

I remember...she came one rainy autumn night, a big mysterious box in her arms. She slipped in and out of every darkened room as quiet as a whisper and then she was gone.

Later, I tiptoed down the corridor, peeping into each room. Tucked inside the arm of every sick, sleeping child was a brand new teddy bear. A path of sunshine!

Not one child would ever know who brought the huggable companion to share his hospital pains. She would have no thank yous, no tributes. Anonymous love. That was enough.

Father, help me to do some unseen kindness today, just for the love of it.

 ## THE RED SCARF

THERE is a little story of love I remember each Christmas. I especially remember it the day I begin my Christmas shopping. It happened years ago on one of those raw December days that make people wish they had shopped in July. Snowflaked winds whipped through the streets. Hunched on a sidewalk bench sat an unshaven man. He wore a threadbare jacket and shoes with no socks. He had folded a paper bag around his neck to keep out the biting wind.

One shopper paused, saddened by the man. *Such a pity,* she thought. But there was really nothing she could do. While the shopper lingered, a little girl, 11 or 12, walked by and spotted the frost-bitten figure on the bench. Wrapped around the girl's neck was a bright red woolen scarf. She stopped beside the old man, unwrapped her red scarf and draped it tenderly about his neck. The child slipped away. The man rubbed the warm wool. And the shopper crept away, wishing she had been the one to give the scarf.

I was that shopper and God taught me something that day. Wherever I am, whatever I possess, there is always something I can give—a touch, a smile, a prayer, a kind word, even a red scarf.

Lord, such as I have, help me to give it.

NOVEMBER

Giving thanks always for all things.

EPHESIANS 5:20

EVERYDAY GIFTS

WE ambled along a dusty path through the woods, toting our fishing poles to the pond. My husband and children threw themselves into the delight of fishing. But I'm ashamed to say I grumbled about the weather, which was muggy; the fish, which weren't biting; the children, who were sliding down a mud bank; and of course the fishing worms, which were… well, worms.

As my misery grew, I escaped to the pine trees beside the path and quietly sulked out of sight. Soon my attention was drawn to the footprints etched in the dust along the trail. My husband's tennis shoe, my sandal, the children's bare feet. I gazed at them attentively and found myself thinking how good it was simply to be able to walk. How wondrous to move through the woods! I studied how big the children's feet were today compared to the tiny feet blotted in their baby books. Then I noticed how our footprints mingled together in the dirt, feeling anew how precious my family was to me, how glad I was for their steps intersecting through my life.

Gratitude poured over me—for woods, health, growing feet and the sharing of lives together. But most of all I felt freshly aware of the Giver. His Presence, which had been so remote all day, seemed to spill out of those moments of praise.

I learned something that day. Buried under our busyness

and grumbling are gifts we no longer see. Small, everyday blessings we take for granted.

Let's take time to praise God during each day for those positive, but overlooked blessings in our lives—music, laughter, memories, books, friends, second chances, orange pumpkins, warm fireplaces and, of course, all the footprints scattered through our days.

Keep me alert, O Lord, to the myriads of
blessings for which I can be thankful, but
sometimes overlook.

 THREE GOOD THINGS

IT was among my son's school papers—an assignment to "name three things you like about yourself." Bob had written, in large fifth-grade letters: "1) I can play baseball real good. 2) I always make 100 on my spelling tests. 3) I am pretty great!"

The little list (especially that last modest self-description) made me smile. How often Bob had heard negative things about himself: "You didn't pick up your room...You aren't nice to your sister...You're forgetting your manners..." It was only right that he should be as aware of his bright side as he was of his darker one.

Then I remembered how aware I constantly was of *my* negative qualities, probing my faults and confessing things about myself that I felt needed changing. Of course that was important. But it was just as important for me to remember those things God had already changed in me—the strengths He had given, the places in me where "grace did abound." So I sat down and wrote three things I liked about myself. And it really did me good.

Why not celebrate yourself today? You're a child of God and you're pretty great!

Lord, I am thankful for the positive things You put
into my life.

THANK-YOU LETTERS

IT was a letter from a man in Indiana. A man I'd never met. It said: "Dear Mrs. Kidd, every week I write a letter of thanks to someone who has helped me in the past week. I learned long ago that gratitude, like perfume, is of no real value unless it's released. So today I write to you. I want to say thank you..."

I hadn't done much. He was expressing thanks for some small published piece I'd written. But as I held his letter in my hand, his gratitude filtered through the air with its lovely fragrance. A warm and special feeling spread through me. The stranger from Indiana was so right. Gratitude should not only be felt but expressed in order to do the most good.

I walked to my desk and pulled out a sheet of stationery. "Dear Mrs. Jones," I wrote, "I just began a practice of writing a weekly letter of thanks. Well, what you said when you spoke at the meeting yesterday helped me a lot. I want to say thank you..."

Help me not to bottle up thank-yous in my heart,
Lord, but release them to spread their warm,
sweet aroma to others. And to You, too.

 # SPECIAL GRACES

ONE day while on a retreat, I told the director: "It's been one of those years. A close friend died, lightning struck our home, our taxes went up and..."

"You remember *those* things very well," the director said with a sympathetic smile. "Now I dare you to write down ten special graces that God has given you in the last year."

"Graces?"

"You know, an undeserved gift from God, some act or sign of His love," he answered.

Well, I never could resist a good dare. So I sat on a bench under a tree and stared at the blank paper. *Ten?* I thought. *That many!* I jotted down a few obvious things. Then slowly I began to remember. All the nice people who had casually wandered in and out of my life. Coincidences. A moment of hope. A shared joy. Tender words when I needed them most. A touch. So many wonderful things! I began to write faster and faster.

Finally I stopped and looked at the pages in amazement. *You did all this, Lord?* I thought. I saw then that the graces of God are often so close to us that we don't see them. We become unaware and take them for granted.

Perhaps God has done more in *your* life too than you know. Go on, get some paper. I dare you....

Keep me sensitive to the exquisite blessings
You give us every day, Father.

 THE SEASHELL

I WAS awakened by a crash of thunder and a torrent of rain slamming against the beach house. The windows rattled and lightning filled the room with stuttering light. Outside, black waves rose up and roared. I lay awake all night, marveling at the fury of nature. Finally near dawn the storm abated.

After breakfast I walked down to the beach. The shore was strewn with beauty: rare shells from far out on the ocean floor, sea-polished pieces of driftwood, rumpled chains of seaweed. I could only imagine the joy the children would have in filling their buckets today.

I bent down and picked up a delicate pink shell. How wonderful it is that such exquisite treasure can come from a squalling storm. Like the storms in my life perhaps? Does God bring something good from them too? Are there hidden treasures in wait in the after calm? Precious peace, untarnished faith, priceless reassurances of His love...God-given gifts?

I carried the pink shell back to the cottage—a reminder to search for the treasure after the storm rather than stare at the heavens and ask "Why?"

Lord, help me discover Your good gifts when the
storm abates.

DECEMBER

*Glory to God in the highest, and on
earth peace, good will toward men.*

LUKE 2:14

 GIFTS OF THE HEART

MY husband and I attended a staff Christmas party at the college where Sandy works. There was to be a gift exchange, but Sandy insisted we didn't need to bring anything.

"We're not giving the kind of gift you're thinking of," he said. "You'll see."

My curiosity was aroused when, after dinner, one by one the employees rose to give their gifts. And indeed they were not anything that could be wrapped up. It cost nothing, yet it was priceless. For each one gave a verbal gift—co-workers looked at one another and out flowed the gifts. One said, "You have been such a help to me, taking the time to listen to my problems." Another spoke of the encouragement the other had given him during a difficult time. There were exchanges of gratitude, admiration, thanks, and praise. There were even tears shared that drew the group closer together.

And I could not help but think that this kind of gift-giving was closer to the spirit of love and sharing than hurried purchases we sometimes make in stores. A heart-to-heart, face-to-face gift of words.

So this year, in addition to the kind of presents which usually crowd beneath our tree, we plan to draw names among our family members so we can each prepare a special gift for one another—gifts of the heart.

This Christmas help me to bestow on someone
I love the gift that is deep within my heart,
dear Lord.

 FROM A SECRET PERSON

"MAMA, was there really a Saint Nick?" my young son asked on Christmas.

"Sure there was," I answered, and together we read the enchanting story about this kind-hearted Christian bishop who was born into aristocracy in the third century....

One night when Nicholas was still a youth, he stole into the house of a poor family. The father had three daughters without dowries or hope of marriage and was distraught over how to continue supporting them. Nicholas, thinking himself unnoticed, deposited a mysterious bag on the table; but the father caught sight of him and gave chase.

As he cornered Nicholas, one of the daughters raced up with the bag, which was filled with gold coins. "What is this about?" demanded the father. Nicholas stammered that he was simply using his inheritance to help the poor, as Jesus asked. But the man was perplexed. "Then why did you sneak in at night?"

"I came secretly because Jesus commanded that when you give to the poor, you should not let your right hand know what your left hand does." Then Nicholas made the man promise that he would not let anyone know where the dowries came from.

And that was the end of the story for my little son and me. Except...on Christmas morning a little white envelope lay under the tree. The inscription read: "To Mama. From a secret person." Inside was a dollar bill—no doubt the "secret person's" allowance. And I could tell by Bob's face that it was a moment of unique joy for him...just as it must have been for young Nicholas so long ago.

In fact, it made me wonder if maybe this Christmas you and I shouldn't become "secret persons" too.

Father, today help me give a gift with my right hand that my left hand knows nothing about.

 FAMILY TREE

ONE of my cherished possessions is an old wooden three-tiered cookie tree passed along from my mother. Each Christmas I hang cookies on it for my children, as she did for me when I was a child. But it has always seemed a shame to use the tree just once a year. So last Easter I pulled it out and suggested we hang eggs on it.

The children were eager. "We could even paint faces on the eggs!" Ann exclaimed.

"And fix hats for them," Bob added.

"You mean make egg people?" I asked, delighted at the idea.

They nodded, and soon we were designing all sorts of "people" for our tree, improvising as we went along. Ann busied herself making an Indian girl with black-yarn braids and a feathered headband. Bob made an oriental boy with lovely dark eyes, while I trimmed a Dutch girl with golden hair and a little white cap.

Bob brought his world globe to the table and gave it a spin. Ann hummed "It's a Small, Small World." And as the hours went by, we added a Russian with a fur hat made from the scraps of an old stuffed animal, a Mexican matador, an Eskimo, an African, and an Arab, complete with headdress.

Finally the tree was full of "egg people" from all over the world. But something was missing. At Christmas we had topped the cookie tree with a star. And at Easter it seemed appropriate to use a cross. So we made one from pipe cleaners wound around with burlap and placed it on the top.

As I gazed at all the races represented on our tree, and then at the cross that seemed to draw them together under one umbrella, I felt old barriers melt inside my heart. No matter how different, we are all brothers and sisters upon this earth.

When my husband arrived home, he asked, "What kind of tree is that?" I started to answer, "an egg tree." But I looked at the cross on top and said instead, "a family tree."

P.S. We've used the tree on birthdays, anniversaries, other holidays, too, like World Communion Day. You just might want to get out your "family tree" for the next special occasion.

Father, may our hearts grow ever wider to receive
all Your children as brothers and sisters.

 WE ARE ALL ONE

ON July 20, 1969, Apollo II landed the first men on the moon. Astronaut Buzz Aldrin requested a moment of silence from ground control in Houston. From his space suit he drew out the carefully wrapped elements of communion that he had brought with him from his church back on Earth. In the one-sixth gravity on the moon, the liquid—the first liquid ever poured on the moon—curled slowly and gracefully into the chalice. Then the astronaut broke the bread and ate it, commemorating the words of Jesus: "This is my body broken for you." And as he lifted the cup to drink, he remembered the promise: "This is my blood which is poured out for many."

Commenting on that rare moment of worship while suspended in outer space, Aldrin later said: "I sensed an especially strong unity with our church back home and with the church everywhere." This first holy communion on the moon reminds me that despite the distance of our differences, we are all one. On Earth. And beyond.

Lord, help us today—and everyday—to bring
people together, not in uniformity, but in unity.

Book design by Elizabeth Woll
Type set in Baskerville No. 2 and Tiffany
Cover design by Bob Pantelone
Cover photograph by Doris Gehrig Barker